True Stories of a Modern Mermaid

A Girl From The Sea Series Book 1

by Deanne Welsh

Cover Design by Janet Hirata Stall.
www.JanetHirataStall.com

Unstoppable Writers books are available at special discounts when purchased in bulk for premiums and sales promotions as well as for fund-raising or educational use.

Special editions or book excerpts can also be created to specification.

For details, contact:
WritingFreedom@DeanneWelsh.com

Unstoppable Writers Publishing:
www.UnstoppableWriters.com

Free Facebook Group for writers:
www.facebook.com/groups/unstoppablewriters

Library of Congress Control Number: 2020903486

ISBN 978-1-7321206-1-7

For anyone who has left home, sought home, or found home and knows what it's like to live straddled between two worlds.

I acknowledge & dedicate this book to...

My parents who are my roots & wings.

My beloved fellow-travelers
Justin, Rachael & Lyndsay.

My husband Jon who believed in our future on our first date and saw me for who I am, the girl from the sea with big brown eyes.

Contents

Introduction

"Where are you from?"

That question not only irritated me but also sent icy shivers down my spine. The last time I was asked that question I was from Germany. The time before that I had no answer. I was a missionary kid and quite confused.

Now I was sitting in a classroom being asked the same question by my teacher. Smiling and attempting to keep my cool yet grimacing inside, I responded, "I'm from Canada."

The true answer was that I was from the sea. I tended to push that fleeting thought of being honest aside, out of habit. I didn't want to explain or get into it. Besides, I felt more like a crazy person if I told the truth when asked that question. It seemed like everyone else could easily answer that supposedly simple question, except me.

I was a missionary kid who had been raised on missionary ships at two different times in my life.

I am from the sea.

Despite the nagging feeling that I was withholding from my teacher and classmates, I told the half-truth, keeping the complete story secret, close to my heart.

My response had been this way for years.

I never wanted to live on the sea. The month after my 13th birthday, we drove away from my home and friends of the last four-and-a-half years in Mosbach, Germany. I attempted to remember the last time we had lived on the sea. The memories of those seven years ran together like watercolors. Only a handful of them had distinct shapes, their edges jutting out in a massive sea of color.

Who am I!?

Instantly, I felt adrift and unconnected.

Where are you from?

The sea.

This is my story and I finally found the courage to tell it.

December 1995
Driving to the Logos II docked in Nantes, France

As I stared out the window of the van, the buildings of every city loomed ominously, like giant watchdogs forcing us to keep going. The glass was cool as I leaned my head against the window, glancing at the forms of my family in the van with me. I didn't cry. I forced the tears to retreat: back behind the throbbing grief lodged at the back of my throat.

The world outside the window whirled by as I stared the dogs down.

I was not a child anymore. I was now an official teen and did not want to live on the sea.

I tried to remember the last time I lived there. Closing my eyes, I conjured up a few sporadic memories.

I slowly remembered the colors, countries, and emotional moments of my past.

Somewhere in Africa

I sat on the back of a rough-skinned elephant with my arms wrapped around my dad's stomach. His arms surrounded my little brother Justin. Scrunched together, we laughed as the prickly hair and dusty dry skin of the elephant tickled our bare legs. Mum held my little sister Rachael behind a low, rickety wooden fence watching and waving as we swayed back and forth, heading towards the far end of the pen.

Somewhere in Asia

I skipped down the gangway as I followed along behind my school mates. Kylie, my best friend, was from Australia. She walked in front of me, her blond ponytail bobbing brightly in the sun. We shimmered from the sunscreen our mums had lavishly applied to our faces, legs, and arms. We looked like mermaids, shining in the water.

Our teachers were already in the van as it pulled up to the front of the ship. We piled in and waved goodbye to our mums, who were leaning over the ship's railing, looking down at us. The van took off and we were on our way to a crocodile farm.

I remember staring into the eyes of a crocodile, shortly after we arrived. He had large white orbs and those dark pupils seemed to stare back at me. I felt sorry for him. He was in a cage and couldn't leave.

Somewhere

When I was seven, the ship was in drydock. Fixing a ship is not family-friendly with all the dust, dirt, stink, and welding. At those times, the mums and kids were packed up into the ship's vans and driven to a place where they could stay for a few weeks. This was one of those times.

I remember piling out of the van upon arrival at our new quarters. The creek was the first thing I saw, and my body instinctively moved towards it to explore.

"Deanne! Get your suitcase first!" I stopped and turned around to obey my mother. After dragging my suitcase to the room assigned to us, I sprinted to the creek. Over the next weeks, my friends and I discovered frogs. We squealed with delight as we chased them. Simon, who was from Germany, had a net and we ran for hours scooping up frogs and then letting them go.

I recall holding a very small frog in my hands. I felt its aliveness kicking against my cupped palms. Kick kick kick. When I opened my hands in the warm water of the creek, the kick kick kick rippled the water as the frog swam away.

New Zealand

Dad lifted me up so I could see over the railing of the ship in order to watch the group of professional tribal dancers on the dock. They were welcoming us to their country.

Grass skirts whirled and bounced as they stomped the ground and shouted.

I leaned forward as far as I could in order to see every detail. The blades of grass in their skirts went swish swish. I could feel the drum beats reverberating through my spine. Their movements mesmerized me and I leaned out even further; Dad's hands tightened around my waist. He whispered, "Not too far Deanne." As I glanced back at him, he smiled.

New Zealand

I held Lyndsay's small body wrapped in a pink baby blanket. She was only two weeks old. I cradled her carefully as I walked the narrow passageway with my mother following close behind. I could hear the ship's generator as I walked into my classroom. Lyndsay is what I had brought for show-and-tell. Everyone gathered round to see what was in my arms. Then the teacher asked my classmates, all 5 of them, to take their seats.

Standing at the front of the class, beaming with pride I said, "This is my little sister and she is mine."

In My Parents Cabin on the Ship

The narrow couch in my parent's cabin was one of my favorite places. I'd sit squished between my friends, watching movies like *The Land Before Time*. The small T.V. was positioned on the top shelf of the closet opposite us. We watched with our chins up and our necks craned in order to see the screen. Mum made us a bowl of popcorn and I relished the salty taste and sound of my friend's laughter.

On the Beach Somewhere in the Caribbean

"I'm sorry. I didn't mean to cut off your leg!" Holding my orange bucket and using my little red shovel, I tried to keep the starfish from crawling out of the pail. My shovel was sharper than I thought.

I ran to show Daddy, "I've ruined him! Is he going to die?" Dad explained that the leg would grow back. He said, "Deanne, everything will be fine if you put him back in the water." I looked up at my dad with a puffy face and tear-stained cheeks and said, "I don't want to look at the starfish I broke." Dad gave me an understanding look, took the starfish from my bucket, and gently hurled him into the water.

I stopped eating canned peaches that day. Their orange hue and soft squish and crunch when I bit down on them, reminded me of the amputation of my starfish's leg. I didn't mean to break it.

Memories

My memories hang loosely together like bulbs from a string of lights. I can't remember when or where they happened or my exact age. Instead, I lived moment by moment a young girl placed in front of an ever-changing landscape of people and places.

As a child, it didn't bother me, this abstract-pieced together life. As I grew older and people began to ask questions about the places I had been, I began to feel like an imposter because I could not remember the details. Had I really been to all the exotic places stamped into my passport or was it just a mirage?

I wondered if others felt the same. How many of us were there, growing up between countries, moving from city to city? I thought of my friend Katje who split her time between her divorced parent's homes, constantly adjusting to two different dynamics.

I have been to many countries, but I do not remember much about them.

People tell me I am lucky: a girl from the sea and growing up on ships.

I never felt lucky.

It felt normal until the questions began. Where are you from? What was your favorite country?

It's hard to pick a favorite country when the memories of them run together.

Mosbach was different.

The memory of the sea grew distant after four-and-a-half years in the same town. When people asked where I was from, I said my parents were Canadian but that I was born in Germany.

I am German.

I remember arriving in Germany. I didn't mind the strangeness, harsh language, or new landscape...even though I was no longer at sea. Changes were normal, like breathing. I was used to being out of place. During my first week at recess, my classmates kept coming up to me and repeating a phrase in German.

I shook my head, unsure of what they were saying.

It wasn't until I told my English friends about it and they translated, "They're asking if you want to play?"

Once I understood, I always said yes.

On the first day of school, I remember walking on the sidewalk up the hill, turning right, crossing a street, and counting the one-hundred-twenty steps we had to climb to get to the street where our school was located. My brother and I walked up those steps every day with our square Schulranzens on our backs, filled with books.

It took years to learn the language, to seamlessly fit in. Eventually, everyone assumed I was German. No accent.

I spoke, thought, and dreamt in both languages, immersed and cohabiting in two worlds.

There was a time when my friend Anne and I almost started throwing punches. She had decided and declared that I was German and not Canadian. "You were born here. You speak German. You live here. You are German!"

I secretly embraced her forceful declaration, relieved that I finally fit in, and yet would have felt like a traitor if I didn't fight for my Canadian heritage to be noticed.

"I am both! Canadian AND German."

Being plopped into a German-speaking public school and repeating second grade aided my fast assimilation, along with my mirroring skills. I let go of the hue and color of the past and immersed myself where I was at this moment in time.

I had four friends who were like me, a language in each pocket: English and German. As the daughters of missionaries, we understood the chameleon law: observe in order to quickly fit in...mirror the language, humor, and the entire culture of the people in your environment. It was easy!

These four friends were my haven. Instead of bringing the diverse pieces of ourselves to our friendship (German, Australian, Canadian, and English), we created a brand-new shared culture along with inside jokes, seamlessly switching from German to English and back again. Our secret circle in the midst of a foreign place that was slowly becoming home. We used our English as a covert code to fuse our connection and keep others out.

The secret name for our group was SKDDR, which was made up by using the first letter of each of our names. We had all come from the sea to settle in Germany. We even began on the same street in two tall apartment buildings before Salome and Kylie moved away.

Salome was from Germany, Kylie was from Australia, Daphne was also from Germany, I was technically from Canada, and Ruth was from England. Only Daphne was in my class. Ruth went to our school but was a grade above us. Kylie and Salome were at the same school and a grade apart. Each of us had German friends in our classes and although we liked them, our bond came first.

We spent hours in the cement courtyard between the buildings. We ran, invented interpretive dances, played with our barbies, and even held a fashion show before graduating to shooting basketball hoops, riding our bikes out of the courtyard headed for town or the river, and talking about boys.

As our van left Germany, I began picturing their faces. Tears filled my eyes and silently streamed down my face. My friends. My very special friends.

I didn't want to go.

My heart was cramping while my head refused to acknowledge the truth that we were actually leaving Germany.

I didn't want this so-called adventure.

Salome's dad had apologized to me before we left. He said he was jealous of our family getting to go back out to sea. That just didn't make sense to me! Why would he want to leave Mosbach to live on a ship?

I wished he would have taken my place.

Questions swirled around me like probing eyes: Will I see my friends again? When? Will I return to Mosbach? If so, when?

The faces from my childhood at sea had all but disappeared. I vaguely remembered them.

Please don't let this be true of my beloved SKDDR. Fear slid into my gut like ice. What if they forget me? Is it possible? They are my best friends. I don't want to forget their names and faces EVER.

My life, like the endless sea, stretched out before me. Long and lonely.

My friends remained behind.

In my mind, I saw them waving from the curbside of my family's empty apartment.

Don't go, my heart cries, even though I am the one leaving.

I have already left.

I whispered inwardly, *Don't cry, Deanne. Don't cry.*

Closing my eyes, I visited the world I was leaving: cobblestone streets in the center of town, and the sound of our shoes as we walked to the ice-café. Our teasing and laughter filling the air. I was the goofy one, often breaking out with energetic dance moves and my loud gunshot laugh.

Don't cry. Don't cry.

The cramps intensified. I wished the pain in my chest would go away.

I focused on my memories.

I thought about my school and classmates. Only a few months ago they had elected me to be their class president, now I was leaving. I'd worked so hard to fit in and this was the pinnacle of belonging, being chosen to lead my class.

I wanted to reach out to them and apologize for leaving, as if it was my fault, as the tears pressed against my eyelids.

Don't cry.

My mouth opened in a silent sob.

Be strong, I told myself.

Your family has enough to worry about without hearing your pain.

You are the oldest. Your siblings look up to you. Be a good example. Hold it in. You are stronger than this. Just stop. The soft breath of my sleeping siblings confirmed that I must be silent. No one heard my thoughts in the dark van. Four small tears cascaded down my cheeks and met on my chin.

I held it in and kept my fears and grief a secret. By the time we arrived, I had swallowed the pain and could hear it whimpering like an abandoned puppy from the pit of my stomach.

Thirteen hours later we arrived at the ship.

Arrival
Nantes, France

"Wake up! We're almost there!" Dad could barely contain his excitement as he drove us through the dock entry gate.

Even though his voice woke us, it was Mum's voice that kicked us into action. "Quick, put on your shoes, we're almost there. Justin, stop poking Rachael and get your shoes on."

As Justin reached for his shoes, Mum turned around to make sure we were moving and rolled on with, "We're almost there! Let's clean up as much as we can! Here's a trash bag. Deanne, can you put those wrappers in it?"

Her voice stopped momentarily when the van did. I crammed my feet into my sneakers, trying not to think. I glanced out the window into the darkness, my eyes hungrily trying to catch a glimpse of the ship.

Our excitement and fear were palpable. We stumbled out of the van onto cramped legs.

Our bodies and minds were groggy and lethargic.

Looking up I saw her, The Logos II. Her name meant, Word of God but she looked more like a pale shimmering mermaid stretched along the cement pier. Her long white body was translucent against the grey of dawn. My breath quickened.

This was my new home.

I heard the ocean gently tapping against the quayside like a soft knock asking to come in. It sounded like laughter and yet all I felt was fear.

We gathered our backpacks and followed Dad up the gangway. I paused at the bottom. The first step felt so final. This is the beginning of my new life and new home. I don't like it, but Mum's voice hurried me forward. How can a simple 13-hour van ride to another country put over a thousand miles distance between me and my life?

"Come on Deanne," Mum called out.

I looked down, afraid of slipping through the holes between the gangway steps, even though my brain knew I was too big. The soft lapping of the ocean floated up to me like fading laughter. Would I be okay? Each wave caused a creak and clunk in the gangway and the dark water below seemed to be whispering secrets into the air.

Was this really going to be my home?

The ship smelled familiar, of oil and salt. I longed to return to Mosbach. My brain kept repeating, *I don't want to live here!*

At the top of the gangway, the watchman on duty welcomed us. He was quite handsome and I thought, maybe it won't be so bad here after all.

Stepping onto the deck, I saw two large wooden doors before us. The watchman headed down the gangway to help with the rest of our luggage. We had given most of our possessions away.

It was incredible how much a driven mom can cram into a single van while still leaving space for her family.

Dad held one of the two swinging doors open. We stepped over a slight ledge into a large rectangular room with worn couches hugging the walls. Another set of wooden double doors was opposite us, leading out to the deck on the other side of the ship.

It's quiet and empty. Where is everyone?

Then I remembered how late it was.

Suddenly a tall man with a thick mustache appeared in the far-passageway. He greeted my Dad in a boisterous voice, "Hello Myles!"

"Harold! Great to see you!" They embrace.

"Patty, kids, I'd like you to meet Harold!"

"Welcome," Harold said as he approached me. I stretch out my hand towards him for a handshake. This is how Germans greet new acquaintances.

"We hug here," he said and wrapped his arms around me for a squeeze.

I stiffen.

Harold hugs each of us and says goodnight.

We were exhausted.

Dad led us to our cabins towards the front of the ship. Doors lined both sides of the narrow passageway. Swinging open a door on our right, "This is the bathroom and shower area that we will be sharing with the others who live in our passageway."

He walks a few steps further down the passageway and opens a second door, "Here's another shower." We peek inside the door and see a tiny room with a shower and countertop.

Continuing, we passed doors on our left. "This is where some of the singles live," Dad explained. There were names on the doors. Shiny squares of plastic with a paper name tag slid through. I read the names and wondered who our neighbors would be.

We were nearing the end of the passageway. There was only one more door on the right and two on the left.

"Rachael and Lyndsay, this is your cabin," Dad says as he opened the door on the right. Mum gently herded them into their room. I stayed in the passageway, peeking in. On the far side of the room, a set of wooden bunk beds was attached to the far wall. There was a worn sink in the corner, a desk with a chair, and a bookcase with only a small space between it and the open door. My heart sank. What would my cabin be like?

We walked a few steps further and Dad stopped at the last door on the left.

"Deanne," Dad looked at me with hopeful eyes. "This is your cabin." I knew I should be happy about having my own space, but everything was so dark, tight, and narrow here.

This is my home?

I stood in the doorway and my heart sank. It's so small. To my right were a desk and chair squished next to a closet that looked like it was holding its breath. The chair came in quite handy every morning when we were at sea; I used it to steady myself when dressing. The bed was a pull-out and when I went to pull it out it almost touched the closet. Directly in front of me, scrunched next to the bed, was a sink partially blocked by a small book-case hugged by the wall.

There was a window above my bed. I prayed it looked out onto the water, but when I knelt on my bed and pulled back the curtains it faced a rusty wall. Evidently, a window with a water view was too much to hope for.

How can my parents be moving us here? This is our home?

The statement contorted into a question. I went to my parent's cabin at the end of the hallway. It was a narrow room with a small desk, sink, fridge, and larger pull out bed. There was a small, single window on the far wall.

Moving the curtains, I glanced out at the deck and sky. The window looked out over the bow of the ship. There was a high wall and railing so my parents didn't have a view of the water either. Their cabin was slightly bigger than mine and later they put two comfy chairs in the space between the pull out bed and the door leading to Justin's cabin, which was like a big closet with bunk beds. Our small video player and TV would be unpacked the following day and placed on a shelf in the small closet, located across from my parent's bed. Their bed was converted to a couch every day.

This is my home.

No, it can't be. I can't accept the statement.

I headed back to my cabin and after changing into my nightgown, I unpacked the rest of my clothes stuffing them into the small closet. Shortly after I crawled into my small bed, Mum and Dad came in to say goodnight, even though it is almost morning.

Mum whispered in my ear. "Have a good sleep; I love you,"

"I love you too," I said.

"I love you, Dee Dee," Dad said as he kissed my cheek.

"I love you too Dad," I whispered, holding back my tears.

Mum flicked off the lights and as the door closed, the tears came. They trickled across my face, leaving a moist circle on my pillow.

I don't want to be here...

This is not my home.

The last thing I remember before falling asleep was the emergency light shining through the window over my bed and the heaviness in my chest feeling like a bubble trying to emerge up through my throat. I kept pushing it down, willing it to stay inside instead of erupting the way it wanted.

Be quiet.

It's not a big deal.

You're okay.

Stop it.

First Day

I opened my eyes and stared at my small room, quietly feeling my way around the space inside me. The heaviness from last night lingered and my chest felt compressed.

I thought about the last time I saw my friends; we said goodbye and hugged for the last time. Ruth held me the tightest. She was the one who wore her heart on her sleeve.

As we drove away, I began to despise the word goodbye. There was nothing good about that word.

I had to be brave. I was the example for my three younger siblings. I didn't want to burden my parents who looked tired and sad themselves, especially Mum. When we drove away in the van, I would never again see my favorite couch overflowing with art supplies and piles of books again.

The last weeks before we left had been filled with 'meetings' with Mum. She went through every single item we possessed and had us decide which ones we loved best.

Everything else was now gone, left behind.

Even some of the things I loved the best hadn't made the cut, like my couch: the old friend whose corner I spent hours curled into as I breathed in books.

The tears were escaping again.

I shook my head, forcing the memories and pain down, down, and away. No, I told them. I must be brave. Surely if God had called us, it should not be that hard.

I pinched my eyes shut and turned my back to the door.

When I heard a gentle knock at the door, I slowed my breathing and closed my eyes, pretending to be asleep.

"Deanne? It's time to wake up," Mum's voice sounded insistent.

Her hand attempted to nudge me awake. I opened my eyes and looked into her big brown eyes from which I had inherited my own. "Good morning Dee. We're going to go down and get breakfast in the dining room. Get dressed and we'll meet you in the hallway in five minutes so we can go down together." She retreated, closing the door behind her.

The last thing I wanted to do was go to breakfast.

I didn't even want to get up.

My body felt heavy and strange, like a metal robot. A part of me thought that if I stayed in bed I would miraculously be vortexed back to my room in Germany, where my art supplies and paper awaited my creative presence.

The room was empty when we drove away. All of our belongings were either packed or given away. My things were gone and I knew that I wouldn't be transported back.

I knew that closing my eyes and staying in bed would not change reality, but I closed them anyway. One more minute.

I swung my feet onto the worn carpet and put on my clothes.

I could hear the doors down the hall open and voices floated through my own door. Standing in front of the mirror, I felt like I was viewing a stranger. My eyes looked different and sad. I couldn't go out like this. I pulled the sides of my mouth up, giving myself a fake grin. Then I brushed my teeth.

Someone was running up and down the passageway. Probably Justin. He loved to run. Opening my door, I greeted my family and proceeded behind them. We were like a line of baby ducks with Mum in the lead.

After entering a new passageway and making a quick right turn, we stop at the top of steep, steel steps.

"Hold onto the railing," Mum advised from upfront.

We obeyed and gripped the stair railing. At the bottom of the stairs, we turned left, stepped over a ledge and entered the dining room through two swinging doors.

It was empty. We had slept in because of our late arrival, and I was thankful no one was there beside us.

A stainless steel buffet station rested against the wall. We grabbed our plates and headed to the cereal and toast station. I wasn't hungry. I knew that Mum would worry if I didn't eat and so I toasted two pieces of bread, buttered them up, smeared jam on them, and walked to the table where Mum and Justin were already seated. Rachael and Lyndsay followed me.

"Every family gets to choose a table to have as their family table," Mum explains. "So this will be our table, and we'll be getting a little name tag to put on the end so people know it is reserved for us."

That makes sense!

In a large room filled with over thirty tables, it made sense that families would get to reserve a space so they could always count on being able to sit together. It was also a great system for moms to be able to keep track of their children and make sure they were eating.

We ate in silence as all of us glanced around the dining hall, soaking in this big room.

Every person on the ship had a job doing things like laundry, cleaning bathrooms, cooking, and washing dishes. Everyone was assigned a station in order to keep the ship tidy and running smoothly. Some people worked in the ministry areas: book store, conference room, or welcoming visitors at the top of the gangway as they boarded the ship. Even those with a 'job' had ministry opportunities assigned to them throughout their 1-2 years of volunteer service aboard the Logos II or when they weren't working.

After depositing our dishes, we followed Mum back up to our cabins.

"Okay kids, I'm gonna give you fifteen minutes to play and then it will be time to get ready for school. Dad is going to take us to your classrooms and introduce you to your teachers. You'll spend the rest of the morning in school and meet me for lunch in the dining room.

I closed my door and sat on my bed. My stomach was churning as though there were little waves lapping around its sides. I wondered what school would be like. I picked up a book. This was my idea of playing. I could leave in a hot minute and go to my favorite places, hide, and get lost in a story with characters like Robinson Crusoe. It felt like I was on a strange island too.

I heard Mum's gentle knock on my cabin door. So much for reading this morning! I fell back in line, this time behind Dad, to discover the school. With my siblings walking behind me, Mum took up the rear.

The ship smelled of oil, salt, and metal; I missed the crisp air of Mosbach mornings.

In Mosbach, we had our own apartment with a big front door. Even our friends had to knock. Once we opened the door and invited them in, they entered our living room.

On the ship we had doors that led directly into our bedrooms, I mean cabins. It felt strange to be living so close to so many strangers. It was so odd to think of all these cabins separated by thin walls and a single door. There were no doorbells or double-locks and the carpeting was worn thin. It felt like we were living in a cheap floating hotel.

When I asked my dad how many people were living on the ship he smiled and said, "There are approximately 180 people living on this ship from over 35 countries." I wondered what they were like.

As we moved forward, I was relieved to see that the walk to school would be easy to remember. It was down the narrow passageway that ran parallel to the long dining room. This passageway went around the back of the dining room and continued around the other side. At the far end, there was a heavy door leading to the book hold. This is where the overstock books for our large bookstore on the main deck were stored.

Books and supplies were shipped in boxes and placed in a huge container that was delivered to the ship. When a container was delivered to the pier, an announcement was made over the ship's loudspeakers for every available person to help bring the delivery into the storage areas. They formed a line of people winding from the container, up the gangway, down the stairs, and along the passageways to the book hold or the food storage area. The boxes were passed from hands to hands, bouncing along with the long centipede of people, until they arrived at their destinations.

Once in the book hold, the boxes of books were organized and shelved. Before the books were brought up on deck to be sold, the boxes were opened so the price stickers could be put on them.

After Dad introduced us to the book exhibition manager, we continued our walk through the large shelves facing each other, stacked high with boxes of books. Dark narrow walkways stretched out to the right and left, like long thin fingers.

A shiver ran down my spine. I didn't like the book hold. It felt like a haunted house with all of the dust and the smell of books. The middle of the book hold was like a dark creepy library. I began to wonder if there were any creepy creatures lurking in the corners.

Finally, we headed down another flight of steep steps and walked towards our classrooms.

The school was located in the belly of the ship. I listened to the dull spinning of the generator through the walls and wondered if I'd be dealing with that noise as I attempted to concentrate on my school work.

As we entered the school, we saw a tiny library on the right. It was full of books squished together on the shelves. The bookcases went from floor to ceiling.

I tried to scan the titles from the hallway.

In Germany, I would ride my bike to the spacious library in the center of town, every couple of weeks, and exchange five books I had read for five new ones. I missed my bike and the chill of a German winter which consisted of rain, fog, and a dash of wet snow that never stayed for long.

At that moment I wished I could have ducked into my new school library and hid away.

Dad knocked on the classroom door across from the library A short blond woman with a warm smile opened the door. "Kids, this is Ms. Lorraine."

"Hello there," she said and then smiled at the four of us kids. Bending down to Lyndsay's level she said, "Are you ready to meet your classmates?"

Lyndsay glanced at Mum and Dad who nodded reassuringly. She took Ms. Lorraine's out-stretched hand. In they went and the door closed behind them.

There was a classroom next to the library. When Dad knocked, a tall slender woman with wild curls opened the door with a grin and boisterously exclaimed, "Welcome! We're so glad you're here!" She quickly ushered Rachael and Justin into their new classroom. The door closed.

I was the only one left. I felt stiff and wide-eyed. I don't want a new classroom. I don't want new friends or a new teacher. Then in an instant, I was bombarded with flashes of my friends in Germany, our classmates, and my teacher.

Random pictures seared through my brain at the speed of light. It was all I could do to choke back the tears wanting to escape. The voice inside was saying, "No. No way. I don't want to be here. I don't want to go to school here. I don't want to live here. I don't want to start over. Please, dear God. No."

I swallowed hard, forcing the voices of my emotions down into the pit of my stomach where I could trust they would stay quiet.

A woman with long curly hair pulled back into a bun appeared in the doorway of my classroom. "Deanne, we're so glad to have you here. Let me show you to your desk and introduce you to your classmates." She had a powerful British accent.

As I stepped inside, I glanced around.

The desks were along the walls. When sitting at our desks, we faced the wall and had our backs to the teacher. Her desk was close to the door. There were pictures on the wall in an attempt to make this dark, gloomy, windowless room a little bit brighter.

I turned and told Mum and Dad goodbye. I gave them both a big hug, swallowing hard once again in an attempt to push down my emotions. Those little devils kept trying to creep out of my throat and eyes.

Mum said, "I'll see you at lunch Dee!" I didn't respond. My head was spinning as my parents walked away and the door closed.

My three classmates stood up to greet me as Mrs. Rachel introduced them, "Deanne, this is Annegreet, from Holland, and this is her brother Luke. This is Frances from South Africa."

Mrs. Rachel had us take our seats and my classmates returned to work.

"Deanne, this morning I am going to figure out where you are in your studies. Then we'll break for lunch. After, we'll continue with a few more tests so I can find the books you will need."

This is the setting for my new life; reality was sinking in.

I attempted a smile, despite the frown and ache inside.

When noon came, I briefly stepped into the library. Filling one side of it was a desk and computer, which everyone had to share. There was a small TV to watch educational videos, which rarely happened.

I let out a little sigh of relief when I saw all of the books.

At least there were books that I could read, get lost in, and feel safe.

So basically the ship's school consisted of a short and narrow passageway with a skinny supply cabinet, a library, 3 classrooms, and a bathroom. There were no windows in any of the rooms. Classes were divided into the Little Kids, Middle Kids, and Big Kids. The teachers were from England. Did you ever study the Queen's English? Yeah, it was like that.

A Formal Introduction

Each face was transfixed on my family as we stood on stage. Even after being on board the ship for over a week, most of the faces still looked like strangers to me. Only a handful had become familiar: the kids, their parents, my teachers and the few people who had sat with us during a meal: specifically Timothy from Britain who had dark curly hair and who in my mind was gorgeous, though I hadn't told a soul. I often dreamt that he had broken up with his fiancé because he wanted to marry me. If only he could see all of the creativity and beauty in my soul I mused.

This particular night I was wearing jeans and my favorite green shirt.

We were all on display. I was standing next to my dad. It was the Thursday night prayer meeting.

Dad introduced our family to everyone. I felt so alone even though I was standing with my entire family in a room full of people. I didn't want to be there. I knew that most of the people looking up at us would say they had been called to the ship's ministry by God.

I sure didn't feel called, I felt forced.

I wondered if my parents felt called or if our move had more to do with Dad's sense of adventure. Either way, I wanted out. I felt like a coin that was lost because it had fallen between the cushions of a couch.

Do my parents even see the effects this move is having on me?

Later that night as I was laying in my bed, I remembered the last time we were prayed for as a family. After a team potluck, we had stood surrounded by the rest of the Mosbach missionary team. They placed their hands on our shoulders, backs, and heads.

My SKDDR girls stood close to me and surrounded me with interlocked arms. Half-way through the prayer, I felt one of my friends withdraw her arms and step away. A moment later, another one did the same. Opening my eyes, I glanced around and I couldn't see Daphne or Kylie.

The other girls and I went looking for them, once the prayer was over. We found them red-faced and crying in the bathroom. I began to cry as well.

We held each other so tightly that night...their hearts protesting with don't leave, don't leave. My heart answering back I don't want to leave, I don't want to leave.

Our crying ceased when we caught a glimpse of ourselves in the mirror.

Puffy eyes and shiny red faces.

We looked horrible! Everyone started to giggle. The giggles escalated into laughter and after we had collapsed onto the floor, we sat in quiet reflection.

The next morning, my family and I got up before the sun and drove down Hilde Kirsch Strasse slowly disappearing in the direction of France and then the sea.

I wish you were all here, I whispered to myself in the dimness of my tiny new room.

My New Life

Luke and his sister Annegreet led the way up the narrow stairs, through the musty 'shiver-inducing' book hold. The boxes towered above us on the large shelving units. We exited into the hallway where the dead-end was marked with a small stately sign on the wall, next to the closed door. It said: Nurses Station.

The hallway ran along three sides of the large rectangular dining room. We could get to the nurses' station by going right or left as we faced the dining room. Today we choose the narrow passage on the right. We heard voices drifting towards us, and sporadic laughter floating above the talking.

Each step we took seemed to increase the volume.

The nervous knot in my stomach had grown. I wondered what might be around the corner? I felt like a character ripped from their story and placed into another. What was my part in this particular story? Was I going to be attacked by a wolf-like little red riding hood or pirates like in Robinson Crusoe?

I felt like an alien. A stranger in a strange new land or island for that matter. I really was stranded on a floating island!

I missed the rhythm and familiarity of Mosbach, my real home: swimming lessons on Monday nights, volleyball after school on Tuesdays and Thursdays, and basketball on Wednesdays. I missed my schedule and my friends. They knew me, they also knew my secret crush and how I got the scar next to my right eye. I missed being known. I missed having a few close friends who knew everything about me.

Walking down the narrow passageway, I began to miss my spacious walks in the woods and having my own bedroom with a large desk, plush couch, and very roomy bed. On the ship I felt like Gulliver, a giant placed into a world for tiny people.

I began to crave space.

My class in Mosbach had over thirty students and now I was in a class of four; plus everything was now being taught in English. Butterflies began to move in my stomach.

Would I be able to remember German after a year here? What about after two years?

English was the language my family spoke and the secret language between my closest friends and me. I could read in English, but there were many words I didn't know. I knew all of the words in German. I wrote stories in German, dreamt in German and German had better words for certain things.

Over the next few years, I slowly lost my ability to think in German.

My dreams went from German to English.

Today there is a small German man who stands in my brain. He starts wringing his hands when I attempt to speak German because he is increasingly flustered and anxious about my American accent and the loss of vocabulary.

Everything is different in this new world. Instead of walking to school in fresh fog-filled air and rain, I am now trapped in a set of passageways, completely hidden from the elements. I missed the trees and the Neckar River.

A twenty-minute walk down a paved street is replaced by tiled and carpeted steel passageways.

From my cabin it only took me two minutes, one if I ran, to get to school in the bowels of the ship.

Mum would meet us for lunch, just like she did on the first day of school. I would follow my classmates up the stairs, through the book hold and down the narrow passageway towards the dining room.

When I'd walk through the swinging doors, it was like walking into a wall of sound, because the room was filled with so many people. The smell of food in the air and the constant motion created a sense of nausea.

My body felt sweaty surrounded by so many people; they were from over thirty-five different countries. I heard languages I didn't understand and broken English in strange accents. The words all swam together. I felt as if I might drown in this vast sea of people.

During the first couple of weeks on the ship, I could tell that even my mother was distracted attempting to soak in the smells, the sounds, and the enormity of this new place. I wondered if this was how bees felt while inside their hive, surrounded by the buzz of everyone else.

I often thought about being back at our small kitchen table with the bench pushed up against the wall, and sliding onto it for our family meals. It felt small, safe, and quiet as compared to this loud bustling room.

Mum would typically shepherd us towards the front, where we grabbed a tray and fill our plates with food; then she'd usher us back to the table, where we sat together as a family.

"Deanne, take a bite. Justin, it's time to eat," she could usually be heard gently prodding us through a meal trying to take our attention from everything around us, back to the food on our plates and the fact that it was mealtime.

At 12:15 p.m. during lunch, a bell would be rung by one of the crew members a few tables over from us. The bell was suspended from the wall. Someone would pick up the microphone and share a few announcements. Then we would all bow our heads and that person would say a prayer, blessing all of our food collectively.

One day a woman prayed in German. Hearing her speak the language of my heart and home, I instantly missed my friends. I wondered if they were walking home for lunch and what they were talking about. My chest filled with emotion. I would have definitely been at a loss for words, English or German if someone had asked me what I was thinking.

After lunch, I walked with my siblings and friends back to our assigned classrooms.

The walk back to class was always done at a much slower pace.

After school, we'd head through the lobby and back to our cabins, near the front of the ship. There were days I'd close the door and feel exhausted. On other days I would grab a snack and take off with one or both of my two friends.

I did my best to decorate my cabin. I initially decorated it with pictures of all of my friends. It hurt when I looked at them, like small sharp stabs in my chest. I gently unpinned them, placing them in the bottom of my desk drawer. Over the next months I replaced them with postcards of places we visited and bible verses.

During my first week on the ship, when I was feeling really low, Mum had shared a verse with me, Psalm 62:8 about pouring one's heart out to God. From that day forward I did my best to do that. I often worried that He got tired of my sadness and complaining so I tried to stay upbeat and think mostly of how to help other people.

I didn't understand that if this was where I was supposed to be, the very place that God had called my family, why was it hurting so much?

If this is where I was supposed to be, I needed to be brave and keep my feelings of sadness at bay.

It was supposed to be exciting living on a ship. People on the ship were from all over the world. They took turns praying for a meal in their own language. It was amazing to hear people praying in words I couldn't understand and to have a sense that God heard them and understood them.

Going on deck and looking over the railing into the ocean was a treat on any given day or night, except when it stormed. That's when things got dangerous.

Watching the landscape appear in detail as we got closer to a new country was more than interesting, it was fascinating.

When writing letters to my friends I painted my new world larger than it was and by the end of the letter, I almost believed it myself. I became good not only convincing others but even myself, that I was fine.

Shortly after supper, I'd brush my teeth leaning over the tiny sink in the corner of my room. After sliding into bed and laying on my pillow, I'd snuggle-in under the covers and whisper, "Goodnight little emergency light."

Mum and Dad would poke their heads in and wish me a good night as well.

One night I dreamt that we were all eating breakfast and my parents started telling us that they had made a mistake. Dad said he hadn't realized how hard this move would be for each of us.

Mum chimed in with the good news that we were returning to Germany and our apartment on Hilde Kirsch Strasse right away. In my dream, she said we didn't have to go to school that day so we could pack and get ready for the journey back home to Mosbach and all of our friends. I woke up smiling, and then it hit me. Yeah. No!

My sisters still had dyslexia. Navigating between an English speaking home and a German-speaking school was too much. We can't go back! We will never go back!

It doesn't matter how much it hurts or how much I don't want to be here.

"We. will. never. go. back."

There, I said it.

No use in expressing my pain, it will not change anything. It will only make things awkward and be a burden to my family.

Hold it in Deanne.

Hide it.

At school, there were moments when I'd forget how sad I was. For example, when I was lost in a story or learning about water cycles: streams, evaporation, and rainfall. If I could only keep my mind busy and preoccupied all of the time.

Settling Down

On the mornings we sat eating in the bustling dining room, I often wished it was our first day on the ship when the dining room was surprisingly empty, except for a few other families.

One day a deep voice came through the loudspeakers expounding on the importance of serving as Jesus served. Upon questioning Mum I found out that the crew members were in their morning devotional meeting, which is what I was hearing over the speakers. These speakers were located throughout the ship.

Announcements were made from a central kiosk, preceded by three musical notes in ascending order, and then you'd hear things like, "Amy Brown you have a phone call. Amy Brown, you have a phone call." After a while, I learned to block out those sounds.

The kiosk contained the phone for making and receiving calls when the ship was in port. There was only one phone line so calls were mainly reserved for emergencies. If you happened to be in the main lobby, which was downstairs from the kiosk, you would see the person who just heard they had a call rush by and leap up the stairs two at a time.

Phone calls were expensive.

After breakfast, we returned to our cabins to brush our teeth. At 8:55 a.m. we all gave Mum a hug and trotted down the hall for the school. My teacher had tested me in math and writing and found out I was ahead of my new classmate Luke who was younger than me and behind his sister Annegreet who was a little bit older than me.

I had learned some new English words and yet found myself missing others. The hardest subjects for me were math and science because of the technical terms, which I only knew in German. Going to school in English was requiring an entirely new level of language proficiency.

Up to this point, I was a mediocre student, falling in the middle of the class hierarchy. Back in Germany, my homeroom teacher would often use me as an example for the Turkish students who had been born in Germany. "See, Deanne moved here when she was in 2nd grade is getting better grades than you. You need to try harder." I would sink into my chair avoiding all eye contact, hating to be used as an example to shame my classmates.

The 'ship school' was different. There was nowhere to hide in a classroom with only 3 other students. If I couldn't figure something out, I could talk through my questions with my Math and Science teacher Mr. Richard or Mrs. Rachel who taught English, History, and Art. If a subject came easily for me I would breeze through it with no need of their attention.

They simply checked off my completed work and gave me feedback.

I had always been competitive in volleyball and basketball. I decided to bring my competitive edge to the classroom. The distance between Annegreet and myself inspired me. She was the carrot dangling before my nose. Unlike a donkey, I did not want to devour her...I wanted to catch up to her, run beside her for a while, and then sprint into the distance way ahead of her...like Eric Liddell from the movie Chariots of Fire. She was a meticulous student and I mirrored her as though playing Simon Says.

What Annegreet did, I did. If she took notes, I took notes. Then as things progressed, if she wrote a page I wrote a page-and-a-half.

Even though I was improving as a student, beneath my drive to achieve were a couple of small, yet disturbing phrases: I'm not good enough. I need to prove myself.

Within a couple of weeks, I had gained on Annegreet and I was learning more than I had in Germany; however my competitiveness had morphed into jealousy. In comparing myself to her, I found myself falling short. The phrase you are not good enough began to take over my brain. It weighed me down.

Annegreet seemed so sure of herself and even looked smarter, which she was. Her hair and handwriting were neater and contained. I wanted to be her instead of myself.

During those days, I felt like an awkward fawn traipsing towards its mother just after being born.

I wanted to return to Mosbach.

We had two breaks during the school day: a fifteen-minute morning break and a forty-five-minute lunch. We were dismissed at 3:30 p.m. During each break and at the end of the day, we gathered our homework and stormed up the stairs. We were not supposed to run and so we speed-walked, propelling ourselves forward, jostling each other for first place until we entered the passageway where we had to walk single file.

In the main lobby, Frances and Lyndall would rush up the stairs past the kiosk while Annegreet and Luke headed towards the passageway that ran parallel to ours, along the other side of the ship. Mum was always waiting for us in her cabin.

Her first question would be: "How was school?"
Our first question would be: "What's for snack?"

After discarding my books on my bed, and eating a handful of gummy bears, which was today's snack, I headed to the Captain's deck where the bridge was located: down our passageway, through the lobby, and up to two sets of stairs. This is the first time I had seen the sky today. I paused and my eyes started blinking to adjust to the bright sunlight.

Then I pushed aside the small gate and walked onto the Fun Deck, a deck in the center of the ship with a fence around it. It holds a small playground and swing set. I hopped on the swing and took a deep breath.

Looking around I once again came to grips with the fact that my world had shrunk.

I thought this move would expand my world and although my new home floats and will sail to many countries, I was now confined to the body of a ship.

In Germany, my world was large. I would ride my bike to many places. I would walk to town, my friend's houses, school, the pool or the canal. My world stretched across Mosbach, Germany, whereas here I was not allowed to leave the ship without an adult.

Suddenly the 180 meters of the Logos II seemed very small. Thinking of Germany awoke the ache inside of me.

I think of my homework sprawled across my bed.

I slide off the swing and wandered listlessly back to my cabin, hoping that no one would see the pain inside of me. Yet I longed for someone to call out to me saying, "Hey! Are you okay? You seem sad."

I wanted someone to help me.

What do I do with all of this pain? How do I make it go away?

The conclusion I came to was that the answer lies in being strong. If I were stronger, it wouldn't hurt. Perhaps this is God's purpose for me, to be strong?

Seeking Space
Oporto, Portugal

Over the next couple of weeks, I searched for a quiet place on deck where I could be still.

On bad days, I would wander from deck to deck looking for a quiet and secluded spot, only to find way too many people. Eventually, I'd return to my cabin frustrated as heck and sob into my pillow.

On good days, I would find an empty deck or a corner. I could be found leaning over the railing or sitting with my back against the ship's white side. I would go into my secret space where I had jailed my pain and I sit with it for a while, the beauty of the ocean washing over me like a healing balm.

Sometimes I even got the opportunity to leave the ship with my family. Complete strangers who treated us like friends invited us to their homes. It felt surreal being in a strange land and dining with strangers in their home. The strangeness of it all began to feel familiar. I wondered if this was how the children of alcoholics felt...the chaos becoming the sought after normal.

One time a farmer wanted to donate oranges to the ship's community. He provided a way for a group of us to go to his orchard and pick them. My family, all kids included, along with three other people from the ship crammed ourselves into the red ship's van, the one with worn seats.

Periodically sounds, like those of a dying animal, emanated from the engine. I did my best not to hear them. I imagined everyone was hoping that we wouldn't stall out and get stranded by the side of the road.

We initially passed buildings, which become sparse as we neared the end of our two-hour drive. Finally we bumped along a short gravel driveway and stopped in front of a farmhouse.

The house was long and narrow, with rectangular windows. It was caked with dust and dirt and a few white patches peaked through like small hands waving through a fence.

When we arrived, the farmer and his wife came out to meet us and showed us around their farm. We could see large pastures with sheep as we gazed past the orchard. The farmer showed us how to pick oranges without breaking the skin. If the skin broke, the orange would spoil.

Justin and I were assigned to pick together and it soon became a race. When we got tired we threw some of the oranges to the flock of sheep grazing in the field next to us.

Only a few of the sheep responded by chasing the oranges and then biting into them. The juice trickled down their chins and they seemed to be grinning a huge thank you to us. *You're welcome*, I smiled back. It was a perfect sunny day and now when I see an orange I know why orange is my favorite color. I think of the orchard with its bright orange bulbs and the vibrancy of that day.

We stopped for lunch and went into the farmer's small house. There was no electricity and the dining area was dimly lit; there also wasn't much room around the table so we sat close together. The farmer placed a large pot of lamb stew in the middle of the table and his wife got us started passing around a basket of a robustly flavored bread. It was a heavy bread and I could almost taste the texture of it.

I had never had lamb before. I sat in that dim room, surrounded by my family in this foreign place, and the experience became forever linked to the taste of lamb. I cannot eat lamb without remembering that particular moment in time.

My favorite night of the week was Thursday night. It was prayer night and the entire ship's company was required to attend. For one night a week, the ship was mine. Quiet and peaceful. I felt a bond with her on those evenings as I walked the empty passageways and decks undisturbed. It felt surreal and spacious.

I would lean over the bow, the wind blowing through my hair and watch as the waves kissed the ship's side. She was pale. I imagined that she looked like a full moon rising out of the dark water. The lights from the land created undulating ribbons of color as they reflected off the water. I'd breathe in, willing my soul to expand and be filled with her beauty.

My hair fell neatly back into place when I'd re-enter the ship.

The aft mooring station was my last stop. This was the area of the ship where the thick, hairy mooring ropes were stored. They were wrapped around large concrete spools.

I would sit on the top of a spool and watch the waves go up and down.

I would imagine a rope stretching from my chest to the land, currently Portugal, and yet I knew that I was not connected to that particular place or country. This reminded me of arriving in France and boarding the ship.

What did France have to do with me? I certainly didn't have any connection with France, in fact I resented her. No, I hated her. I had to leave the life I loved, and go to France.

Why? It didn't feel fair; going to France felt like going to jail.

The day we left France, I was in my classroom in the belly of the ship. We heard the ship's horn blow and the teachers gave us permission to rush from our classroom and stand on deck.

Looking over the railing of the ship, it felt so strange to be caught between two places. For example Germany and France as well as the pier and the sea. It reminded me of when I saw the Logos II caught between the pier and the ocean. I remember hearing the ocean waves crashing against the other side of her.

As we headed into open water, I looked out into the ocean; then stared back towards the shore, and watched everything get smaller and smaller. The air was brisk as we moved further and further away from the French shoreline.

I noticed the dark grey muddy water. Ugly and yet oddly beautiful as it moved with the swells and swirled round and round. This is what it will be like, the good and the bad of it all.

Daily Rhythms & Feelings

Life on the ship had a rhythm. We got up at 7:30 a.m. and headed to the dining room, returning to our cabins by 8:30 a.m. to brush our teeth. I was grateful that I didn't have to share a sink like Lyndsay and Rachael as I did in Germany. I often heard them arguing when our cabin doors were open, their high pitched voices echoed through the passageway.

After gathering up our homework from the day before and a quick hug from Mum, we'd head down the hall towards our classrooms. If we left any later than 8:55, we'd run.

The steps from our deck to B Deck, which was close to the dining room, was my favorite part of heading to school. I'd skip down them, place my hands on the side of the door frame and swing around the corner, through the door opening, and into the passageway.

Periodically I would bump into someone coming in the opposite direction.

After school, I would hang out with Annegreet and Frances. We'd swing on the Fun Deck, watch movies in our parents' cabins on small T.V.'s or play card games. There was not much to do on the Logos II.

I missed riding my bike and being involved in sports. I had wanted to be a volleyball star and would spend hours in my room and in the courtyard, by our apartment in Germany, improving my skills.

Now that life no longer existed.

On the ship I spent a lot of time in the main lobby, sitting on one of the large couches along the wall, talking with my friends, and watching people. This was the central point of the ship and every couple of minutes someone would walkthrough. When I was alone, I liked how I could sit on a couch, blend into the wall, and still be able to say hi and smile at people when they made eye contact with me.

One day Annegreet and I were sitting in the lobby when we heard music coming from the main meeting room. We decided to explore. After sneaking up the stairs, we entered the back of a darkened room. The stage was lit and we could see some of the ship's crew leading worship. Every seat was filled and I could taste the expectancy and joy in the room. By the time we got there, people were standing and singing loudly to worship songs.

Suddenly I thought of all the stories in which people had crowded around Jesus. So many people wanted to see him that one time, four of his friends had cut a hole in the roof just to be close to him. Sweeping my eyes over the crowd, I suddenly understood the ministry of Logos II. It was about bringing Jesus to the world. In other words, bringing him closer to them.

My pain started to make sense. Perhaps God was hurting me for the good of other people. *I'm here for God, my parents are here for God, and all of the people who come onboard to worship services want more of God.* I never saw this kind of passion in Germany, let alone in myself.

God, maybe you do have a reason for me being here after all.

During those first few weeks on the ship, I often felt as though I was watching myself from afar. Questions of doubt would swirl around in my head.

Am I really living on a ship?

Is this really my life?

How will I ever explain it if words fail me and I can't verbally explain it to anyone who hasn't experienced this way of life before?

Urgency began to emerge to be able to capture this unbelievable, impossible life on paper.

Letter writing became an anchor of my daily life.

I loved letter writing because I could find out what my secret crush from Germany was doing. There were plenty of cute boys on the ship as well. It was hard not to be distracted. My favorite was Robert. I kept forgetting where he was from, mainly because I hadn't visited there yet.

He was shy and his smile was slightly crooked.

Robert sat with my family a few times for dinner. He usually asked a few questions, then fell silent unless he was asked a question. He reminded me of Germany because he came from a small colony, like the Mennonites. My parents had grown up in a Mennonite community and they also spoke German. His English was good, even though he had a German accent. He also spoke Spanish.

Robert worked as a carpenter on the ship and I often wondered what it would be like to fix and build with my hands. His hands were strong and calloused, there was often dust and dirt under his nails. In my mind it made him look rugged.

He liked to tease me and my friends. Robert attended the Scottish dances with us and whenever I danced with him, I could feel my heart skip a beat or two. He was very handsome.

Family Holiday

I enjoyed writing to my friends about our adventures away from the ship. We did some crazy things on those family outings. Our holidays would begin with a van ride, leaving the Logos II behind. In Germany, we didn't go on many family holidays. Most likely because we had the space of an apartment to ourselves as well as the weekly outings to go hiking or walk to town.

On the ship, even though our cabins were grouped together at the end of a passageway, there always seemed to be people around. The cabins were small so we preferred not spending extended amounts of time in them unless we were watching TV.

Once the rhythm of ship life took over, we would take a family vacation every three or four months.

Recalling our first family holiday, I can see us waving goodbye to our driver Rodrigo who was from Chile. As Rodrigo took off down the street, we turned and headed into our hotel. We looked more like a family ready for a hike as we trekked into the lobby with our backpacks and one suitcase. The lobby was spacious, like a breath of fresh air. As Dad proceeded to check us in, I wondered if we could just stay there forever. When I walked into the adjoining hotel rooms, I felt like I was walking into a palace.

The beds were enormous and there was plenty of floor space. I picked my side of the bed and laid my backpack next to it. We spent the next day-and-a-half reading, watching T.V.(mostly cartoons) and taking baths. There were no bathtubs on the ship.

The first night at the hotel my siblings and I got into a fight about who got to take the first one.

Mum decided we should take our baths from the youngest to the oldest. Go figure.

When I complained, Mum gently pulled me aside and said, "Deanne, you're the oldest and so I expect you to be the most mature and to wait patiently." UGHHH! It's not like I picked to be the oldest.

Why do eldest children get the worst part of the deal? Parents seem to think the oldest child is more mature and patient? Just because I'm quiet on the outside, doesn't mean I'm happy about it on the inside. If Mum could have seen my internal scowl, I would have been spanked!

Watching Lyndsay operate from her loud tenacity made me wonder if I should change my strategy. She always seemed to think she had a right to have her way, and being the youngest she got her way more often than I did.

I picked up my book and settled myself on the bed. This could take a while, especially with Justin who would read an entire book while he's in the tub. When he emerged from the bathroom, I barely recognized him. His fingers and toes were wrinkled. He looked more like a prune than a brother.

"Finally!" I exclaimed.

I gathered my PJs and entered the steamy bathroom. I locked the door and filled the bathtub, watching the new steam merge into the steam that was still hovering in the room from Justin's bath.

The next day we headed to the beach. It was a rather cool day; the sand was cold so we left our shoes on. We were wearing shorts and sweaters. Flat stones of different shapes were strewn across the sandy beach. As I picked them up there remained a shallow dip created by their weight. When the thin waves swept over them, their rather dull surfaces would shine with hues of orange, grey, and purple. Further away from the water's edge, the stones, out of the reach of the waves, were less exuberant.

Lyndsay was climbing onto each bench we passed.

Justin and Rachael were competing to find the best stone.

I wandered along, staying close to my family, lost in my own thoughts.

Suddenly I heard Dad's voice, which pulled me out of my head. "Do you want to Deanne?" It took me a moment to register the question, and visually take in the man standing by the parachute.

"Maybe!" I said.

Dad encouragingly replied, "You should! It looks fun!"

I tilt my head back and watched a green parachute drift far above the water. My stomach did a small flip as the word "Okay" came tumbling out of my mouth.

Dad negotiated the price. The next thing I knew, I was standing on the beach with a parachute laid out in the sand behind me. Once again I was trapped, this time by a harness with ropes.

The small boat began to speed away. I watched as the ropes tightened in front of me and with firm pressure on my back, I was lifted into the air.

I rose quickly as the parachute expanded. I held my breath as the earth fell away. My family began to look like tiny ants with stick arms, waving at me from below.

The quiet surprises me.

The wind caressed my hair just like when I leaned over the railing of my new home. At that moment, I decided that I'd rather live up here, build a flying house, and live amidst the wind and the calm. It's the perfect calm that calls to me.

I floated like a bubble on a string. The boat was far below.

I watched the sparkling water, which looked as if a million stars had fallen into it and were floating on its surface, blinking up at me. I breathed deeply, savoring each impression like the last piece of a chocolate bar.

The end came far too quickly. As the boat slowed down, the wind lowered me back to the sand where the salesman grabbed me by the waist ensuring a soft landing. I was breathless and couldn't believe that I had just been in such a wonderful place. I tried to describe it to my family, my words fell short. Why does language fail me when I try to communicate? Especially when I attempt to share the things that are the most important to me.

Our First Christmas

Our first Christmas on the ship felt really weird. We didn't have enough money to do Christmas shopping as we did in Germany. My siblings and I drew names. We each wrote our name on a piece of paper. Then we put that slip of paper into a bowl. Dad held the bowl up high so we couldn't look inside. We took turns reaching into the bowl and pulling out a name. That name represented the only person we'd buy a present for when we went Christmas shopping. Mom and Dad would be getting us each something as well.

When the day for Christmas shopping arrived, I climbed into the backseat of the van with Justin. We usually sat next to each other because he and Lyndsay annoyed one another too much.

When we finally arrived at the store, Mum and Dad had two of us kids wait on one side of the aisle while they took the other two and checked out at the register. I had drawn Rachael's name and so I bought her some Legos. Once the shopping was done, we all piled into the van. It had only taken us about an hour-and-a-half to complete our Christmas shopping.

Christmas included a caroling night, a dress-up dinner, and a brunch on Christmas Day as well New Year's Day.

On Christmas morning my family sat in my parents' cabin to open presents. It was slightly too warm from all of our body heat. We were crammed together with our small fake Christmas tree. It was weird not having a large living room and apartment building to roam about. I still had the smells of the previous year's Christmas within my senses. I could smell Mum's cooking in the kitchen and I was thinking about all of us baking cookies together.

After opening our presents, we retreated back to our rooms as it was too crowded for all of us to be in our parent's cabin at one time. If we had been in our apartment in Germany, we would have lounged around the living room reading our new books or playing with our new toys. We would have stayed together and enjoyed the day.

Today we had gotten ready for a special breakfast and enjoyed the buffet which consisted of pancakes, fresh buns, and other goodies.

After breakfast and in an effort to make this Christmas feel a little more normal, Mum had us help her put together marshmallow Rice Krispie bars. They were a family tradition. Each of us helped to add the ingredients and stir the mixture together, except for Dad he was the photographer.

We crammed into their small non-ventilated pantry kitchen. Mum set the stations up so we each had something to do. There was a plate with shiny forks and marshmallows, a pot with melted toffee and a smidgen of milk, a large green bowl filled with Rice Krispies, and wax paper was set out for cooling the treats. A second plate was there for the finished product. As Mum set up, I carefully stirred the melting toffee and added a smidgen of milk.

Once everything was set up, everyone took their places so we could begin. First, I stabbed a marshmallow with a fork and then passed the impaled marshmallow to Mum who dipped it into the toffee. She made sure it was completely covered, then tapped the handle of the fork on the edge of the pot. Mum handed the fork with the coated marshmallow to Rachael, who gently lowered it into a green bowl of Rice Krispies.

Rachael then picked up a handful of Rice Krispies and pressed them onto the toffee, making sure the marshmallow has been fully coated. Then it was Justin's turn. He ran his fingers down the forkhead, forcing the marshmallow onto the wax paper. Mum was in charge of carefully placing them on the plate. As we continued our assembly line, Justin periodically licked his fingers because the toffee and Rice Krispies had caked them.

I could be heard saying:

"That's gross!"

"Justin! Mum!"

"Justin is licking his fingers!"

Mum just kept calmly telling Justin to wash his hands.

Then we'd all stand there waiting for him.

"Hurry up Justin!" was the impatient cry of all three of his sisters.

He would take his own sweet time, carefully licking each finger and savoring each of the Rice Krispies by chewing slowly. He usually only made it about 5 minutes before his next licking break. Sometimes Rachael and I would join him. His job was the stickiest.

Reaching her max, Mum finally said, "No more licking until we're all done! I don't want the toffee to get hard," she had a stern look on her face. She was a mom with clear boundaries.

Dad stopped in for a couple of minutes to take some more pictures. Years later, each Christmas represented in our photo-albums had a rice-crispy treat assembly line picture. He didn't stay as long as the small pantry was pretty hot. We would have opened the door to the passageway, but that might have set off the fire alarm, like the time we had made toast with the dial turned up a little too high.

Another tradition of Christmas was the care package Grandma Rempel sent each year. She usually sent it a month or two early, which is why we always had it in time for Christmas. Along with the presents, it always included our favorite foods from Canada: Cheerios and Mac N Cheese.

The days of Christmas ran together. We walked into town from the ship with our sweaters and jackets on to see the Christmas lights. They were bright against the chilly darkness of the sky. Nothing else stands out in my memory of that time.

Letters

Onboard the ship I anxiously waited for the mail, hoping it would arrive before Christmas. It didn't. Some very special letters arrived a couple days before we sailed to the island of Barbados. On Friday the 26th of January, 1996 I could be seen clutching eight letters addressed to me. I rushed to my cabin and quietly closed the door. I sat on my bed, curled my legs, and placed the pile of letters at my feet.

I picked up one of the envelopes and held it carefully like a rare jewel. I read the address: Ruth...Mosbach, Germany. I used to live there. Now my mail arrived at the head office and was shipped to wherever the ship was ported. The mail came every two or three months in a large crate, which was then sorted on the ship way too slowly as I anxiously awaited its final destination...my hands.

Gently turning the envelope I opened it with my index finger, leaving a jagged tear. I poured over each letter, relishing the stationery, handwriting, and words from my friends.

Ruth had the neatest handwriting and she had drawn creative borders around her writing. Her letter was the longest. I had saved it for last, knowing that she would fill me in on the many details of life in Mosbach.

Kylie had torn two pages from a magazine and had written boldly across the colorful images with a black sharpie. How creative. I'll have to try that sometime. Salome and Daphne had written their letters on graph paper, the paper with the small squares that we used in school. Salome had included a simple picture of a heart, a frog (her favorite animal), and had drawn a flower next to her name. Daphne and I had been in the same class and in her letter, she had mentioned how our homeroom teacher Mr. Hoffman and some of my German friends were doing. She wrote I miss you, Deanne. Our English class is still boring.

I smiled thinking about the jokes and notes we'd pass to each other. We were far beyond the other students so we were always bored.

With every word, I missed them more. That is why I had taken their pictures off the corkboard in my room.

It hurt too much.

I cried so hard after reading their letters. Then I got into a dialogue with God.

It hurts God!

Help me!

Please help me!

Why God?

Couldn't you have picked someone else? Why me?

I'm obviously not strong enough.

I took a deep breath.

Be strong Deanne.

I'm trying.

I almost start crying again, but decisively push the pain away.

No more crying.

"Okay," I replied.

Taking a washcloth, I wiped away all the traces of tears.

After the pain settled back into the room of its keeping, I placed the letters on the corner of my desk next to a pad of writing paper. I had already begun my replies in my mind.

When I sat down to write, I made a point to carefully answer each question. I also asked many in return. As I read what I had written, I felt that my letters fell short of what I really wanted to say. My mind saw holes between the words. Once again words had failed me. Despite this truth, I bravely dropped my reply letters into the outgoing mail slot.

I went back to my cabin and headed straight for my desk. I carefully placed the letters from my friends into separate colored folders, each one neatly labeled with their name.

Eventually, the folders grew thick with their correspondence.

Writing letters to my friends gave me a voice, although not everything in them was true. I continued to leave out the loneliness and pain. I wrote about cute boys and the cool experiences I was having, like the day I went parasailing. The emotions I shared in that particular letter were completely true. I really could have lived in the calm of the sky, floating with the birds forever.

Receiving and sending letters made it easier to convince myself of the good in my life. They helped me survive. Without them, my existence was caught in a deep dark cloud of longing for the past.

From Homesick to Seasick
Departing Portugal in Europe
for Barbados in the Caribbean

We were set to depart at 4 p.m. The gangway was raised at 3:45 p.m. and I watched the men who worked at the port stand ready on the quayside. At 4 p.m. sharp the captain sounded the horn, a deep disturbing sound that reverberated across my skin and down to my toes. The men bent over the thick mooring ropes and lifted them off the steel cleats, tossing them into the water. SPLASH! The deckhands pulled the ropes up, wrapping them around the metal spools of the aft mooring station. Leaning out, I watched the small tug boat pull us away from the port.

Goodbye Portugal. Goodbye Europe.

We are already in choppy water as we head out to sea. My new home, the Logos II settles into continuous movement, swaying against the waves that rush past her sides. I leave deck to distract myself with a book. The thoughts of leaving Portugal, reminded me of leaving Germany. I do my best to move the pain I feel inside out into the open water. The waves grow choppier as I read and I soon feel pressure in my head. I hope I don't get sick.

"It's time for supper, Dee." Mum pokes her head into my cabin.

"Okay!"

We walk to the dining room, stopping briefly at Rachael and Lyndsay's cabin to gather them. I'm finding it hard to walk. I begin to feel as if I'm in a daydream. My body feels as though it's flying. Then my feet are gently lifted towards the sky. The next moment it's as if I am being slowly lowered toward the floor until it feels as though a giant hand is pressing down on me. Am I a bird being flattened to the ground by a lunging cat?

I stumbled awkwardly down our passageway towards the main lobby, surrounded by the sound of a creaking ship. I struggled to keep my balance.

Entering the dining room, my stomach turns as I smell the food. Ugh. I don't know if I can eat anything. Moving to our table at the back of the dining room, away from the smells coming from the buffet table, I begin to feel sturdier. I decide to have two pieces of toast with a thin layer of butter. Eating helped and by the end of the meal I felt better. Maybe I can live on a ship after all.

Once everyone had finished supper, I went on deck to spend some time with my dad.

Everything seemed so dark. The lights from the land were already far away and shone brightly like small stars. The wind was cold and after freezing the image of the dark night in my mind, we went inside. The smell of the aging ship, mixed with steel and a hint of oil, had already begun to smell like home to me.

I got ready for bed early that night. Carefully balancing myself with one hand on the back of my chair, I changed into my PJ's and crawled into bed still feeling slightly nauseous. The creaking was loud and incessant. As the ship lurched from side to side, I imagined myself in a giant cradle with the great watery hand of the sea rocking it. I really just wanted the persistent motion to stop so

I could fall asleep. Sleep continued to elude me for several more hours into the night.

I woke up a few times as the boat continued to lurch. This was not what I had imagined. Before I had left Germany, my mind had created a romantic picture of the ocean; calm with a gentle breeze, soft swaying motion, and dolphins jumping out of the water as they followed the ship. Last night had been the complete opposite.

It was terrifying to think of such a giant expanse of water just outside the hull of the ship. If the sea decided to, it could capsize and pull us all to the bottom of the ocean in a flash.

I closed my eyes and listened to the pipes hanging from the ceiling in my cabin, pulling against the metal hangers that held them. Just like when I was walking to dinner, the Logos II created alternating sensations as I laid in bed.

First my feet would rise and I would feel my head being pushed along my pillow towards the wall. I was afraid that my head would slam into the wall from an especially strong wave.

Then suddenly, without warning, my head felt light as my feet were gently moved down towards the end of my bed. Back and forth. Back and forth.

I longed for stillness.

It was now morning. Mum's head poked in and she could see that I was awake.

"Hey Dee. It's time to get up." Her voice was cheerful and yet she sounded tired. Her looks matched her tired voice.

I made a face.

"Come on. It's time."

I sat up once she had closed the door and I instantly felt dizzy. I laid back down. I don't want to get up. Slowly, knowing that Mum would return any second and be angry if I wasn't up yet, I sat up once again, swung my legs over the side of the bed, and lowered my feet to the floor. Attempting to balance myself with one hand on the back of a chair, I got dressed.

I could hear Mum in the hallway coaxing Rachael and Lyndsay and then Justin to get up and get ready for breakfast.

The pressure in my head had subsided and now my stomach felt a bit queasy. I walked into the dining room and headed straight for our table.

I looked at Mum and told her that I wasn't very hungry.

She made a plate of toast and coaxed me into eating a piece. After breakfast I headed back to my cabin and quickly brushed my teeth.

The bathroom felt claustrophobic.

I headed to the aft meeting room with my siblings. Our classroom had been relocated to the back of the ship. We could hardly study in our usual classrooms, in the bowels of the ship, with all of this motion. The aft meeting room was one of the more stable areas of the ship. This was the room where conferences were held. There were large windows and each class had their own group of tables set up with space in between them.

I spent most of the day attempting to concentrate and being distracted by the view. The windows I faced reminded me of looking through sandglass as the water completely covered them. Watching the line of the water going up and down was mesmerizing.

The extra chairs had been stacked and tied against the wall in order to keep them in place. I imagined the utter chaos of the ropes breaking and the chairs flying across the room. *I sure hope that doesn't happen.* I kept reminding myself that the ropes were strong.

As soon as school got out, I rushed to my cabin, tossed my homework in a messy pile on my bed and went on deck.

During our voyage, I spent my days either in school, on deck or in the lobby. The lobby was near the middle of the ship and thus felt more stable.

The first week at sea, I felt like I was in survival mode. It was all I could do to choke down dry toast and function at school.

On my worst day that week, I threw up seven times. Each time I felt better. By the third time, there is nothing left in my stomach. By the seventh time, I was exhausted and Mrs. Jennifer excused me from school for that day.

I stumbled into my parents cabin to tell my Mom and then headed to my cabin, depositing my queasy body across my bed.

It's true. At first, I thought I would die leaving home and now I wished I would.

Being seasick is no joke.

The second week as my body adjusted and the sea became calmer, I started to fall in love with the rocking motion of my sea cradle. At night, I listened to the dull drone of the generator. It was as constant as the water we floated upon.

The thing I still wasn't used to was how claustrophobic it felt being out at sea with 180 people in one small vessel. To alleviate the boredom of being stuck on a ship with no place to go and nothing to do besides talk, write or read, the Logos II's leadership scheduled movie nights twice a week.

There were two locations where we could view a movie. The large main meeting room or the smaller aft meeting room. For our first movie night, my family had chosen the aft room. I arrived shortly before the movie began. Dad had situated the chairs so that we had one to sit on and one for our feet. It was better than going to a theatre, which I had only done once while living in Germany.

Everyone was quiet taking in the drama of the movie. Every now and then the entire room would erupt in laughter. I knew most of the crew by face now, and smiled or said hi when passing them in the narrow passageways. I didn't talk with any of them. I talked to my family, teachers, and friends. There was a deep layer of myself, my emotions and my thoughts, that I did not share with anyone. Tonight, for a moment, I forgot my loneliness as I sat surrounded by the bodies and sporadic laughter of those on board. It felt like I was part of a big family and I felt alive. I had a sense of real connection as we floated across the ocean that night.

I am not alone.

Every culture has its own sense of humor. Years later when I attended college, my intercultural communication professor said that the hardest part of a culture to pick up on and adjust to is their humor.

After the movie was over, Mum herded my siblings towards the stairs to go back through the ship to our cabins.

Dad and I wanted to walk outside. As we stepped over the slight ledge, moving through the doorway, and onto the wooden deck, the cold wind tingled our skin. A few minutes later I started to shiver. We turned to walk down the deck but stopped.

A large silver moon was resting above the ocean.

Stunned, we paused at the railing to soak in the iridescent glow of moonlight and the pathway of silver laced waves below.

My breath catches. My heart quickens. I could have missed all of this if we had stayed in Germany.

Thank you, God.

I know I was supposed to see this, a gift from you to me. A precious jewel that I was meant to find.

I stand beside my Dad until the cold gets the best of both of us.

We walked quietly into the main lobby and headed towards our respective cabins. There were no words for what we had seen.

"Goodnight Dad."

"Goodnight Dee. I love you."

"I love you too."

I hugged him tightly and then we parted.

Choosing A New Identity
Sailing from Portugal to Barbados

There were reasons I did not belong to each of the countries I lived: you are not German, you have a Canadian passport. You are not Canadian, you've only lived here for a year. Even though you were born in Germany, you didn't live here a full 5 years in order to be recognized as a German citizen, blah, blah, blah.

The sea was different. She was voiceless and so I did not fear her rejection. She was accepting of me. Her ever-changing shape and color validated my nomadic story. She seemed to be searching and reaching like me. For years I felt she had chosen me. If not, then God.

Perhaps God had chosen me.

Since leaving Germany, I began to ask questions about things I took for granted. The pain I had experienced felt like I had failed God. However, if God was actually perfect, I was a failure of my parents. I started to feel like I couldn't trust any of them. I would never admit this and I was ashamed to even have such thoughts.

I began to place the responsibility for safety and comfort on myself.

If I was experiencing this type of inner pain, surely my siblings must be too. I anointed myself their protector, not just against physical harm, but against any kind of harm or pain. I began to treat them nicely and try to be a part of their lives, investing my attention and energy in them.

I became a third parent a parentified child of my own choosing. Without a lot of conscious thought, I began to criticize the choice of my parents to return to the sea. In fact, I sometimes felt critical of other choices they had made and were continuing to make.

I tried to protect my siblings from my parents choices by making myself into a buffer, to explain and comfort.

I gave up my childhood to supposedly save my siblings. I thought this was the purpose behind the pain God was inflicting upon me.

I believed that He was making me stronger by having me give myself and my energy away to others since I was not important.

The sea became my metaphor as the world I knew dissolved. It was there that I lost and found myself. I exchanged my selfhood for her wisdom: be adaptable, gently push against the shore if you must, but it will not make room for you.

Your strength lies in your silence and even if you speak, you will not be heard.

I stare at the endless sea.

She waits for me and I stand spellbound, enraptured by the vastness of her shape and movement. The crests of her body rise and fall like hands reaching for the sky only to fall away. I lean on the ship's railing, my eyes drifting hungrily out over her vastness and ever-changing shape.

Disconnected.

Alone.

The curves of her surface dance and in her, I find meaning beyond words. Her beauty gives me hope that there exists a world beyond my pain.

Be strong, Deanne.

Be beautiful.

If you are strong enough, you will be beautiful and loved.

Don't tell anyone how hard you find it to be strong.

The ocean was silent.

Next to her, I feel small and insignificant. The vastness of the world outside of Mosbach and the many people I have met confirms to me that I do not know as much as I thought I did. All the opinions I had about the world, along with the places and people that defined my place in the world, have been uprooted.

You are not important, the voice stated.

"I know," I replied.

I'm not sad. It is simply true.

At that moment, I saw myself as a tiny speck on the deck of a ship in the middle of the Atlantic ocean.

I wanted to lose myself in her beauty and to forget all the pain. I felt myself slipping into nothingness.

I imagined the ropes that connected me to each of my friends and to Mosbach; they were stretching thinner the further we sailed and the longer I was away.

Perhaps being from the sea would be okay. There is an abundance beneath the swell and surf of the ocean.

Shall I surrender myself? Everything will be okay - or will it?

The calm clear crystal ocean glitters. I look with burning eyes and a seared heart.

Maybe it is time to let go…

I was tired of all the ropes in my chest, pulling my heart in so many directions. Tired of the hope of finding a home and having that wish remain unfulfilled. My story was already confusing: a Canadian living in Germany. Born in Germany, yet not a German citizen.

Finding her, the lady of the sea, I found the answer to my dilemma.

I am not from Canada. My passport may be Canadian, but I am not.

I am not from Germany even though I was born there, lived there for over four-and-a-half years, and could speak and dream in German.

I am from the sea.

There it is. Solid. Strong.

All the ropes binding me to the land have been let loose and I am now afloat.

I am from the sea.

It fits and suddenly I feel calm. This is who I am.

She is beautiful, strong and fluid, all the things I aspire to be.

I have lived here the longest and now I have returned.

I am from the sea.

Abundance Beneath the Sea

The first half of the voyage the water was grey and choppy. As we moved towards the Caribbean, the water lightened and we saw fish. Sailing towards the sun, the crest of each wave sparkled like a million diamonds. I did not want to feel the sadness and grief anymore. Instead of letting my feelings go or crying them out, I had pushed them into a secret room and into the darkest corner of that room.

I started to believe that a new season was going to begin.

It's time to smile.

During the second half of the voyage, I spent more time in my favorite places on the ship. I liked to lean over the bow and watch from the front of the ship as it sliced through the water with the billowing waves rolling away from the ship.

One day, I was on the side deck watching the waves move in crescendo and decrescendo. Small silver bodies began erupting up out of the waves. Wings stretched wide until they disappeared into the body of another wave.

I stared in disbelief.

A fish with wings? How cool!

I spent many hours during this voyage, watching the seemingly weightless bodies of these bird-like fish shoot out of the water, flutter their wings, then soar on the breeze from the salty spray of breaking waves. Eventually they'd tuck in their wings and dive back into the water.

The side railings of the ship had a thick wooden ledge. When I'd lean my elbows on them the small salt crystals, dried by the sun, left small indents on my skin. My usually fine hair would become thick from the salt in the air.

At night my favorite place was the aft mooring station. I would sit on the large coils of rope and watch the swirl of disturbed water that the Logos II was leaving in her wake. Occasionally, a patch of algae far below would be stirred up by the disturbance and rise up to flash a fluorescent green from an underwater world of shifting color.

Being close to the water became my new obsession. I started leaving early for school so I could be alone. Watching the ocean put me into a meditative state. This ritual became a great way to start my day because there was nothing but water. Sometimes I would see the faint shape of a ship far away. The vastness and beauty of the sea assured me that everything would be okay. I relaxed in her presence as she surrounded me.

On the tenth day of our voyage, while I was doing an assignment in the classroom, there was an exciting announcement that came over the loudspeakers.

"There are dolphins on the starboard side of the ship. Repeat: There are dolphins on the starboard side of the ship."

Finally!

I jumped out of my chair, knocking it over. The entire school, kids and teachers, created a stampede as we moved towards the starboard deck. Upon our arrival, we leaned over the side of the ship.

"There they are! There they are!" I pointed in disbelief.

A school of dolphins was swimming three meters from us. I waited for them to jump. They didn't. I watched their gleaming backs and fins rise and fall in the water like the chest of someone breathing as they slept. I imagined swimming with them, my body gracefully gliding through the water, the sun warm on my back, and then cooled by water. They were flawless.

I must tell my friends about this!

Pieces of my identity were floating into place. I am from the sea, like a flying fish or a dolphin. Yes. Even a mermaid. Although I still felt lost, I had found my true home. The sea.

The water would clear and we would see the dolphins again.

The dolphins and the flying fish were everywhere as though welcoming me home.

The sea is my home.

The sea is me and I am the sea: sparkling, full of hope and aspirations. Perhaps one day the sea will rise in me and my voice will be free.

A Note From The Author

Our identity rests not in the opinion of others,
rather it hinges on two things:
who we think we are
and
who we choose to be.

Once I was no longer running away, I was free to hear and move into the truth of my story. I am now the author of four books: the one you hold in your hands, *Story By Story*, *When God Calls A Writer* and *Living with Dragons*.

Writing this series of my memoirs scared me for years, but I knew others had similar stories. If I held back, the power of this book would be muted. As I wrote, I laid my soul bare, wide open for the world to see. I know what's it's like to feel stuck and even trapped by the emotion and power of a childhood experience.

These days there are plenty of resources regarding HOW to write and IMPROVE one's craft. HOWEVER, since the emergence of self-publishing, there is an increased pressure from traditional publishers for writers to have an email list and an online presence.

I have a quick question for you?

Do you write? If so do you write as a hobby or are you more interested in getting your work out into the world, changing lives, and creating an income? Either way, I launched Unstoppable Writers in October 2017 with the sole purpose of providing support and community for writers regardless of where they were on their writing journey. What began with less than five members has become a fierce and loyal tribe of committed writers, enthusiastically encouraging one another, and celebrating each other's successes.

As Unstoppable Writers, we believe that there is a place for EVERY writer. We spit out the poison of comparison and thinking that we must step on other people in order to get ahead. We celebrate the success of others and are committed to creating a life-giving community of writers as artists.

Are you ready to catapult yourself and others to success? If so, here's the Unstoppable Writers mantra...

My passion fuels me.

My persistence is a superpower.

My productivity allows me to shine.

I am committed to making powerful connections that will propel me forward.

I know that my writing serves a greater purpose.

Perhaps you need God to whisper this to your soul today: As a writer and artist, it's easy to get hung up on what everyone else is doing, or how your work compares to what already exists. When we silence our minds and pause, we know the truth.

We were made to create, write, speak, sing, dance, and paint. Whether you are 'simply' living and creating your life, which is a feat in and of itself or in the midst of a creative project, my prayer for you is that you will find the courage and soul-freedom to release your pictures and stories onto the page and into the world because I know, deep in my bones, if the message is burning within you - someone else needs to hear it too.

If you are longing to connect with other committed writers, I invite you to join our private **Unstoppable Writers Facebook group** here...

www.facebook.com/groups/unstoppablewriters/

Quotes from Deanne Welsh on creativity and courage

As creatives, we are caught between two worlds: the visible and invisible. There is often external pressure to explain our compulsion to create and capture the ideas swimming in our soul and imagination. In an interior world of vibrant color and powerful presence, it is normal to experience discouragement when our actions and accomplishments do not match the potency and power of our expectations.

What I want for you is empowered confidence to set your ideas and stories free.

Embrace the process, edit away and don't forget that it is you who decides when to stop and start... EVERYTHING!

Sing off-key, scribble rather than draw, write with your worst grammar. Life is meant to be enjoyed. You are not a machine required to produce a perfect product. People will buy you, not your books, so connect with your audience and attract more followers, I'll show you how.

My prayer for you is that you would find the courage and soul-freedom to believe your worth and release your pictures and stories onto the page and into the world because I know, deep in my bones: If the message is burning within you - someone else needs to hear it too.

Courage comes when we take the next step.

Other Books by Deanne Welsh

Living with Dragons

When God Calls A Writer

Story by Story

About The Author

Unstoppable writer Deanne Welsh energizes her clients to finish and publish their books. She is a mind-reading marketing maverick and author who empowers her clients to express their soul story with clarity, creating magnetic messaging and a powerful online presence.

Raised on missionary ships and writing since she was seven, Deanne is an author, speaker, and marketing strategist who equips writers to create a step by step plan to optimize their time, energy and resources. She is also the Managing Editor for a Christian marketing agency and previously served as the Manager of Customer Service for a million-dollar nonprofit.

Deanne enjoys the Arizona sun with her sweet 5-year-old Eli and her husband Jon.

Connect with her at DeanneWelsh.com on Facebook @deannewelshwrites or Instagram @deannewelshTV.

If you are a writer, join her free Facebook group for writing advice and to connect with other Unstoppable Writers @unstoppablewriters.

Made in the USA
San Bernardino, CA
27 February 2020

65078337R00054